The Story of
TENNIS CHAMPION
ARTHUR ASHE

The Story of
TENNIS CHAMPION
ARTHUR ASHE

by **Crystal Hubbard** with illustrations by **Kevin Belford**

Lee & Low Books Inc.
New York

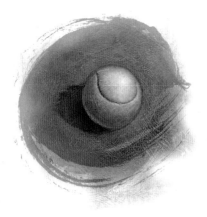

Text from *Game, Set, Match, Champion Arthur Ashe* copyright © 2010 by Crystal Hubbard

Sidebar text by Crystal Hubbard copyright © 2018 by Lee & Low Books Inc.

Illustrations from *Game, Set, Match, Champion Arthur Ashe* copyright © 2010 by Kevin Belford

Photo credits:
p. 13 © Can Stock Photo Inc. / mhprice
p. 21 Keystone Pictures USA / Alamy Stock Photo
p. 31 © zhukovsky / 123RF Stock Photo
p. 49 Peter Jordan / Alamy Stock Photo
p. 50 © instinia / 123RF Stock Photo
p. 67 Associated Press photo by Ron Edmonds © 1992 The Associated Press
p. 69 ZUMA Press, Inc. / Alamy Stock Photo

LEE & LOW BOOKS Inc., 95 Madison Avenue, New York, NY 10016
leeandlow.com

Edited by Jennifer Fox and Cheryl Klein

Book design by Charice Silverman
Book production by The Kids at Our House
Manufactured in the United States of America by Lake Book Manufacturing, Inc.

The text is set in Volkhorn.
The display font is set in Avenir.
The illustrations are rendered in acrylic and Photoshop.

10 9 8 7 6 5 4 3 2 1

First Edition

Cataloging-in-Publication Data is on file with the Library of Congress.
ISBN 978-1-62014-789-4

*To Dr. Paul Schultz, who embodies
the heart, generosity of spirit, and
intelligence of Arthur Ashe — C.H.*

*For Earl and Rita's kids,
and all kids at heart — K.B.*

TABLE OF CONTENTS

CHAPTER ONE

TENNIS DREAMS

Arthur hugged his big wooden tennis racket to his chest. He was watching a young black man practicing on the Brookfield Park tennis courts in Richmond, Virginia. The man was good—as good as any of the players Arthur had seen at Byrd Park on the whites-only courts. There, Arthur could only watch from a distance as coaches instructed their students.

It was the early 1950s, and tennis facilities in Virginia were **segregated**, separating blacks and whites. Blacks were allowed to play at Brookfield, and for Arthur this park was home. He and his younger brother, Johnnie, lived here with their father, Daddy Ashe, the special officer in charge of the park's eighteen acres. Arthur's mother had died when Arthur was just six years old—the same age he was when he'd found the big, old wooden tennis racket and started carrying it around everywhere he went.

WHOOSH! With one smooth swing of his arm, the young black man sent a **forehand** shot sailing into the opposite court.

I wish I could do that, Arthur thought.

Arthur kept watching. Finally the man finished his practice and began to pack up. He had noticed Arthur too, and came over. "I can't tell if you're dragging that racket or if that racket is dragging you," the man said.

Arthur smiled shyly in response. He was used to people teasing him about being thin.

Then the man asked him a question. "Would you like to learn to play?"

"Yes, I would," Arthur said quietly.

The man Arthur met was Ron Charity, one of the top black college tennis players in the United States. Soon, Ron started giving Arthur lessons. He taught Arthur how to grip his racket; how to hit forehands and **backhands**, the powerful ground strokes that send the tennis ball back and forth over the net; and how to serve with speed and **precision**.

Arthur's arms and legs were as skinny as soda straws, but he was strong and had quick-fire reflexes. He soaked up everything Ron taught him, including the rules of the game. Arthur learned that tennis matches were divided into sets, that sets were divided into games, and that it took four points to win a game. He learned the odd scoring system that went *Love, 15, 30, 40* instead of *0, 1, 2, 3.*

Scoring in Tennis

Players flip a coin or spin a racket to decide who'll serve first and from which side of the court he or she prefers to serve. The flip winner might also choose to leave these decisions to his or her opponent. Whoever serves first will do so for the whole game.

Servers start the game by standing just behind the baseline, anywhere between the center mark and the singles sideline on the right. The server has two tries to get the ball over the net on every point. The serve must land in the opponent's service box, which is diagonal to the server, with the ball bouncing once before the opponent returns it. If the ball misses the opponent's service box, the server serves once more. The server loses the point if the service box is missed on both tries. If the ball touches the net yet tips into the proper service box, the serve doesn't count. It's called a "let," and the server gets another chance to serve.

Once the serve goes in and the opponent returns it, players volley the ball back and forth until someone hits it into the net, hits it out of bounds, or misses it. If

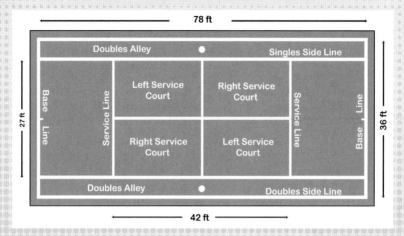

Diagram of a standard tennis court.

the person who makes the mistake is the server, the opponent gets a point. The server gets the point when his or her opponent errs.

Tennis matches are divided into "games" and "sets." There are six games to a set, and three or five sets in a match. Games are scored starting at zero, which in tennis is called "love." (Tennis was invented in France, where the French word for "egg" is *l'oeuf*. An egg looks like a zero, so some historians believe that English players mispronounced the word, leading to the term "love.") After love, the first point is 15, then 30, then 40, then game point, which wins the game.

If the score is tied at 40 ("40–all"), that's "deuce." To break the tie, someone must win two points in a row. The back-and-forth to win by two points can go on a long time.

Once a game ends, the other player serves. After odd-numbered games (Game 1, Game 3, or Game 5), players switch sides on the court. The first player to win six games wins a set. As with deuce, a set must be won by two games. If one player has won six games and the other has won five, the player with five must win three more games to win the set. If the score ties at 6–6, a tiebreaker is played.

The match is determined by the best two out of three or three out of five sets.

Arthur was eight when he entered his first tournament at Brookfield in 1951. Playing with his heavy secondhand racket, he lost his first match to an eleven-year-old. But Arthur enjoyed competing, and he continued to enter tournaments at other blacks-only parks.

Arthur started winning, and his confidence grew—a little *too* much. In a match against a child his own age who was less skilled than he was, Arthur blasted shots past his opponent. Arthur's serves were so fast, the other boy swung hopelessly at the tennis balls streaking past like comets. Every time Arthur won a point, he looked around to make sure everyone had seen it.

After the match Ron was upset.

"But I won," Arthur said, confused.

"You're supposed to play your opponent, not play up to the spectators," Ron told him. "If you ever show off like that again, I won't coach you anymore."

Arthur was ashamed. He never **gloated** or showed off again, not even when he beat older, stronger players and won Brookfield's annual tennis tournament. Soon, Arthur was so good that Ron began taking him to the Richmond Racket Club, a private tennis club for blacks, to play against adults.

CHAPTER TWO

DR. JOHNSON

By the time Arthur was ten, he was ready for more **extensive** coaching. Ron and Daddy Ashe arranged for Arthur to spend summers at a tennis camp at the home of Dr. Robert Walter Johnson in Lynchburg, Virginia. Dr. Johnson was a medical doctor who loved the sport and was active in the American Tennis Association (ATA), a group formed in 1916 to allow African Americans the opportunity to play.

Dr. Johnson was also a good player. He had won several mixed doubles ATA titles with his partner and former student, Althea Gibson. Arthur knew that Dr. Johnson built champions. It was hard for Arthur to leave his family, Ron, and Brookfield; but if Ron and Daddy Ashe thought Dr. Johnson's camp was best for him, Arthur would respect their decision.

Still, Arthur had problems when he first arrived at camp. Dr. Johnson had a very different coaching style than Ron. Ron's approach was one-on-one, with Ron tossing and hitting hundreds of balls to Arthur to improve his game. Dr. Johnson had more structured training. Arthur was just one of several students there, and they used equipment to sharpen their skills.

Arthur had won lots of matches playing Ron's way. He didn't want to do anything differently. He began to act out and did not listen to Dr.

Althea Gibson

Althea Gibson was an African American tennis player who became the first person of color to win a Grand Slam title, the 1956 French Open women's singles. Gibson went on to win eleven Grand Slam tournaments in her career, and was one of the first nine inductees into the International Women's Sports Hall of Fame.

Gibson was born in Silver, South Carolina, on August 25, 1927. Her parents were sharecroppers, which meant they farmed land that belonged to someone else and gave the owner a share of their earnings. When the Great Depression **befell** the United States economy in 1929, sharecropping no longer provided a livable income. Gibson's family moved to Harlem in New York City. Their neighborhood was roped off during the day so children could safely play organized sports. In 1939, Gibson earned the title of New York City women's paddle tennis champion. Two years later, Gibson entered her first tennis tournament, the ATA New York State Championship. And she won! Gibson won the girls' ATA National Championships in 1944 and 1945. She lost the women's final in 1946 but recovered in 1947 to win the first of ten straight women's titles.

With Dr. Walter Johnson as her mentor, Gibson competed in bigger competitions. She attended Florida A&M University on a tennis and basketball scholarship, graduating in 1953. She then concentrated on tennis, going on to win fifty-six singles and doubles tennis titles in her **amateur** career. This includes her eleven Grand Slam titles, six of them in doubles. She was the first African American tennis player to compete in the French Open, Wimbledon, and the US Nationals (renamed the US Open in 1968), as well as the first to win all three. She ranked number one in the world in 1957 and 1958—the years she won both Wimbledon and the US Nationals—and was voted Female Athlete of the Year by the Associated Press both years.

Gibson retired from amateur tennis in 1958 and from professional tennis in 1964. When most white players retired from professional tennis, they earned a living through paid **endorsements** for products such as athletic equipment, shoes, and clothing. Gibson wasn't offered major endorsements because of her race. Denied the opportunity to earn a living in tennis, the thirty-seven-year-old Gibson became the first African

Althea Gibson with her first Wimbledon championship trophy, 1957.

American woman to join the Ladies Professional Golf Association (LPGA) tour. Racist country club officials often refused to allow Gibson entry into competition, and she frequently had to dress for tournaments in her car, since she was banned from clubhouses. She nonetheless managed to be one of the LPGA's top fifty money earners for five years running, but because she was barred from so many tournaments, her lifetime golf earnings never topped $25,000.

Gibson retired from professional golf in 1978. She died on September 28, 2003, at the age of seventy-six, from complications following two infections.

Johnson. Frustrated, Dr. Johnson called Daddy Ashe, who traveled three hours to Lynchburg to talk to Arthur. Daddy Ashe was very strict, but also loving and fair. He listened to Arthur's concerns, then explained, "Ron taught you everything he could. He is the one who thought Dr. Johnson could teach you even more. Dr. Johnson is teaching you now. You do everything he says."

Arthur never defied his father. After their conversation, Arthur dedicated himself to training Dr. Johnson's way. Arthur studied Dr. Johnson's books about tennis. He sharpened his coordination using a short stick to hit a ball suspended by a string and used a special stand to practice thousands of serves. A Ball-Boy machine spat thousands of balls for Arthur to hit. He hit ground strokes against a backboard.

Dr. Johnson's neighbors complained about the *thumpity-bump* of Arthur's hard shots against the backboard at seven in the morning, but nothing could stop Arthur from practicing. Arthur realized he could hone his skills and keep winning by training Dr. Johnson's way.

Over the eight years he trained with Dr. Johnson, Arthur won many titles and tournaments, competing in Virginia and other states. It didn't matter who was on the other side of the net: bigger, stronger, older, black, or white. The skinny kid with glasses unleashed blistering serves that made his opponents think their rackets had no strings. Arthur made winning look easy because he practiced so hard.

The United States began changing in the late 1950s. Segregation was being challenged in the US Supreme Court, and race relations were sometimes tense. Dr. Johnson knew the only way his young black players would succeed and earn the public's respect was if they were **courteous** and self-disciplined. They had to be dignified always, no matter if their opponents cheated or if people called them names. Dr. Johnson taught Arthur the importance of carrying himself with calm and dignity on *and* off the court.

By Arthur's senior year of high school, Dr. Johnson and Daddy Ashe realized that Arthur would have to make another change if his skills were to improve further. Arthur needed to play tennis all year, not just in the summer. Richmond had no indoor courts for blacks, and segregation still kept Arthur off the courts for white people.

Dr. Johnson had an idea. Arthur could move to St. Louis, Missouri, to live with Richard Hudlin, a former captain of the University of Chicago tennis team. In St. Louis Arthur could play year-round. Arthur talked it over with Daddy Ashe. "I'm used to being away from home," Arthur said. "Imagine how much better my game will be if I can play all year."

Arthur was no longer a little boy, and his father respected his opinion. "I guess you're going to St. Louis," Daddy Ashe said.

In St. Louis, Arthur competed against top players. In addition to playing outdoors, he began to play indoors at places such as the 138th Infantry Armory, where he expanded his game to new court surfaces.

> "Imagine how much better my game will be if I can play all year."

The armory's polished wood floors were slick and fast, and they helped Arthur learn to react more quickly to shots. He trained himself to hit the ball on its way up from a bounce rather than when it was coming back down. This gave his opponents less time to prepare for the return.

Before, Arthur had always played from the baseline at the back of the court, relying on powerful forehand and backhand shots to send the ball over the net. The armory's faster surface forced Arthur to change his style of play. He began running up to the net after his shots to meet his opponent's returns with volleys—quick shots made before the ball can bounce. This fast, **aggressive** style came to be known as "serve-and-volley," and Arthur was one of the first to use it.

CHAPTER THREE
COLLEGE ACHIEVEMENTS

Arthur graduated from St. Louis's Sumner High School in 1961. He had the highest grades in his class, but it was his tennis skill that earned him a scholarship to the University of California, Los Angeles (UCLA). It was the first scholarship the school had ever given to a black tennis player.

Arthur was the twenty-eighth best amateur in America when he began at UCLA, but the school had lots of good players. Arthur was the team's number-three player behind Charlie Pasarell and Dave Reed.

As part of the college team, Arthur felt a sense of belonging. He was eager to compete against other strong teams, but Arthur quickly

discovered that he still wasn't welcome to compete everywhere. The UCLA team was invited to a tournament at the Balboa Bay Club in Newport Beach, California, but the club didn't want Arthur to participate. Blacks were not allowed at Balboa Bay. Arthur's friend and teammate Charlie, a native of Puerto Rico, refused to play in support of Arthur. UCLA coach J.D. Morgan wanted to keep the whole team home, but Arthur asked him not to. Arthur thought it would be better to take such a stand at another time, when it mattered more.

Arthur didn't allow the Balboa Bay Club **snub** to hurt his game. In his second year at UCLA he earned a chance to play in the championships at Wimbledon. Along with the Australian, French, and United States championships, Wimbledon was a Grand Slam tennis competition, one of the sport's biggest and most respected tournaments. Winning enough matches to qualify for Wimbledon was easy for Arthur. The hard part was figuring out how to pay for the trip.

Grand Slams

The Grand Slam tournaments, the four most important annual events in professional tennis, are comprised of the Australian Open in mid-January, the French Open in May and June, Wimbledon in June and July, and the US Open in August and September. Also called "the majors," the Grand Slam tournaments offer players the most **ranking points**, prize money, and public and media attention, as well as the most talented pool of competitors.

Each tournament is played over a period of two weeks. The Australian and US tournaments are played on hard courts, the French is played on fast and slippery red clay, and Wimbledon is played on grass. All the tournaments feature several events: men's singles; women's singles; men's, women's, and mixed doubles; and wheelchair categories. In all nonmajor tournaments, men and women play best-of-three sets to determine a winner. In major tournaments, men play best of five. (There remains an antiquated notion that professional female tennis players lack the **stamina** and endurance to play five sets of tennis in the majors.) In wheelchair

South African tennis player Lucas Sithole competes in the 2013 US Open.

tennis, matches are best-of-three sets.

The term "Grand Slam" originally referred to the achievement of winning at least one event in all four major championships in a single calendar year. A non-calendar year Grand Slam occurs when a player wins at least one event in the four majors in a row, no matter the year the major was played. Winning an event in all four majors at any point during the course of a career is a Career Grand Slam. Winning the gold medal at the Summer Olympic Games in addition to the four majors in one calendar year is the "Golden Grand Slam."

Only seventeen players in the history of tennis have completed a Career Grand Slam. The most recent players to achieve it are Serena Williams, Maria Sharapova, Roger Federer, and Rafael Nadal, each of whom won their fourth consecutive major in 2012. Don Budge, Maureen Connolly, Rod Laver, Margaret Court, and Steffi Graf are the only tennis players to have earned the elusive calendar-year Grand Slam. Graf is the only player to have won the rarest of Slams, the Golden Grand Slam. In 1988, she won all four majors and the Summer Olympic gold medal in women's singles. With twenty-three singles titles through 2017, Serena Williams holds the record for most Grand Slam wins in the modern competitive era, including two non-calendar year Grand Slams.

A woman named Julianna Ogner solved the problem. After watching Arthur in an exhibition match at the California Club in West Los Angeles, she approached him. "You're a remarkable player," Mrs. Ogner told Arthur. "What are your plans for the summer?"

"Playing for the Wimbledon championship, if I could get to London," Arthur said.

Mrs. Ogner offered Arthur the money he needed to make the trip. Arthur was speechless. All he could think of to say to Mrs. Ogner was "Thank you."

Mrs. Ogner was a stranger and a white woman too. Her generosity helped heal some of Arthur's pain at being excluded from Balboa Bay.

Wimbledon was a whole new world for Arthur. When he called Daddy Ashe from London, he had so much to tell him about the All England Lawn Tennis and Croquet Club. "The umpires wear hard straw hats and **carnations**, just as they did in 1880," Arthur said. "There's green everywhere—green ivy, green canopies, green doors and balconies and chairs."

Arthur carried his excitement to the courts. Using his serve-and-volley game, he beat his first opponent in **straight sets** and made it through the next round as well. In the third round Arthur faced American Chuck McKinley, the top player in the United States and an old rival from the junior circuit. Chuck was too good. He beat Arthur in straight sets and went on to win the men's singles title.

Arthur was disappointed, but he'd made a good showing in his first year at Wimbledon. He

had learned a lot about playing on grass courts. Grass slowed the tennis ball. The uneven surface caused the ball to make funny hops and taught Arthur to move quickly on the balls of his feet and chase down the ball no matter where it bounced. Wimbledon also gave Arthur the chance to meet players from all over the world. He saw how a sport could bring people together.

Back in California at UCLA, Arthur kept competing and winning, all the while maintaining the schoolwork and grades to keep his

scholarship. On August 1, 1963, he won a place on the United States Davis Cup team. The Davis Cup is the biggest international event in men's tennis, and Arthur had been a Davis Cup fan his whole life. No black man had ever been named to the American team, and Arthur was delighted to be the first. He took pride in his chance to play for his country.

In his first Davis Cup appearance at Cherry Hills Country Club near Denver, Colorado, Arthur beat Venezuela's Orlando Bracamonte in straight sets, helping the United States win the championship.

Over the next few years, Arthur continued to play and win on the college tennis circuit. His successes made his hometown of Richmond proud. On February 4, 1966, the city that had once kept him off many of its courts because of his skin color honored him by declaring Arthur Ashe Day. When Arthur spoke at the ceremony, he said, "Ten years ago this would not have happened. It is as much a tribute to Richmond and the state of Virginia as it is to me."

A few months later, Arthur graduated from college with a degree in business. He had led UCLA to the national collegiate tennis title and was the top amateur player in the United States.

CHAPTER FOUR
THE US OPEN

The "open era" of tennis began in 1968. That meant professional players were now allowed to compete against amateurs such as Arthur. Five national tournaments were combined into one main event, the US Open.

When Arthur entered the first US Open championship in September, he faced the best players in the world—not just the best amateurs. Arthur was completely focused, and it served him well. Match after match, he advanced, beating both amateurs and pros. After defeating South African Cliff Drysdale in a quarterfinal match and fellow American Clark Graebner in the semifinals, Arthur was on his way to the finals.

On September 9, Arthur walked onto the court at the West Side Tennis Club in New York. This was one of the biggest matches of Arthur's life. It would not be easy, but he was ready. Arthur knew his opponent, Tom "the Flying Dutchman" Okker, well. The two had a long history of competing, and Arthur had bested Okker in their last two encounters: the quarterfinals of that year's Wimbledon tournament and the US Nationals just a month before. Now the Flying Dutchman wanted revenge.

As the match began, tension was thick in the air. In the first set Arthur and Tom took no chances. The two fought game for game. Neither was able to get ahead and win by the necessary two-game lead. Arthur's powerful serve was hard for the Flying Dutchman to handle, but Tom wasn't going to give up easily. Finally Arthur served two aces—unreturnable serves—and won the first set, 14 games to 12. The Flying Dutchman battled back to win the second set, 7–5.

Relying on his big first serve, Arthur won the third set, 6–3. Tom countered by taking the fourth set, 6–3. The two men were now tied at two sets apiece. Whoever won the fifth and final set would be the champion.

With Daddy Ashe and Dr. Johnson in the stands watching, Arthur's concentration and **anticipation** increased. As the two players struggled for the win, Arthur led the fifth set by two games. All he had to do was keep playing his game—serving hard, rushing the net, and placing shots out of the Flying Dutchman's reach.

Tom wanted to win as much as Arthur. He played hard, using his speed and clever shot placement to win points. But Arthur was a smart player. He studied his opponents' weaknesses. Tom's was his backhand. Arthur knew better than to **exploit** an opponent's weakness throughout the whole match; that might help his opponent strengthen his flaw. Instead, Arthur waited for just the right moment.

Arthur's patience paid off. He began hitting to Tom's backhand, and dominated the final game. With the score 40–0, Arthur only needed one more point to win.

Arthur served for the match. The sound of his racket strings striking the ball echoed like a small cannon. Then he sprang to the net to meet the Flying Dutchman's return shot and volleyed the ball out of Tom's reach.

Arthur won the final point and his first Grand Slam event. His fists clasped high in the air, he stood proudly as the first US Open champion. Always the good sportsman, Arthur shook Tom's hand after the match. Then he turned to see Daddy Ashe hurrying onto the court. Arthur was so happy with his victory and so proud that his father had been there

to see it. Usually reserved, Arthur threw his arms around his father and hugged him right in front of everyone.

Even though Tom Okker lost the tournament, as the highest-finishing professional he received the $14,000 prize purse. Arthur, an amateur, couldn't accept anything more than a $28-a-day allowance for his expenses. Arthur didn't care about the money. He wanted to keep his amateur status so he could stay eligible for Davis Cup play.

"It's nice to hear the announcer say, 'Point . . . Ashe,'" Arthur said. "But I'd rather hear him say, 'Point . . . United States.'" As much as he cherished winning America's national championship, Arthur preferred to win *for* America, in the Davis Cup competition. Three months after his US Open victory, Arthur's dream came true. He and his teammates beat Australia to win the Davis Cup.

His US Open and Davis Cup wins made

"It's nice to hear the announcer say, 'Point ... Ashe.' But I'd rather hear him say, 'Point ... United States.'"

Arthur very famous. He began playing all around the world, and he stood out everywhere he went. At twenty-five, he was the number-one player in the United States and the only elite black player. Six foot one and just one hundred sixty pounds, he was so tall and skinny that people said he looked like a bow and arrow when he arched to serve a tennis ball.

CHAPTER FIVE
GOING PRO

In 1969, Arthur decided to become a professional. He'd achieved all he could as an amateur and wanted to earn a living as a tennis player. With little **fanfare**, he gave up his amateur status and began his professional career, winning the Australian Open for his second Grand Slam victory.

When Arthur went to newsstands, his own face looked back at him from the covers of *Life* and *Sports Illustrated* magazines. *The New Yorker* published a story about him. Coca-Cola and American Express wanted him to represent their products, and Head USA sporting goods created a racket called the Arthur Ashe Competition. The quiet, skinny boy from Richmond had grown into an international star.

Not comfortable just soaking up the spotlight,

Arthur decided to use his fame as a tool to help other people. On a television show called *Face the Nation*, he said, "Prominent black athletes have a responsibility to champion the causes of their race." Arthur became active in getting young blacks in America interested in tennis, and he helped form a union for tennis players.

Through tennis Arthur had become a champion around the world, and he felt strongly about giving

"Prominent black athletes have a responsibility to champion the causes of their race."

back on an international level too. Growing up with segregation in Richmond, Arthur knew how wrong and hurtful it was to be separated because of one's race. He found a cause fighting apartheid, South Africa's official policy of keeping black and white people apart.

Over and over South Africa denied Arthur entry into the country to play tennis, but Arthur kept trying. He won the support of US Secretary of State William Rogers, the United States National Lawn Tennis Association, the South African Lawn Tennis Union, and South African players such as Cliff Drysdale. With help from people around the globe, Arthur got South Africa expelled from the Davis Cup competition in 1970. He brought worldwide attention to South Africa's unfair apartheid policies.

In 1973, South Africa relented and allowed Arthur to play in the South African Open. He won the men's doubles title playing with his former opponent Tom Okker. Arthur was proud that his name—a black man's name—would join a list of champions in South Africa.

Apartheid

Beginning in 1652, the land that became the country of South Africa was colonized by Dutch and British invaders. These settlers instituted policies that limited governmental participation and land ownership by the native African population.

South Africa won its independence from Great Britain in 1934. When the all-white National Party gained power in 1948, it launched a system of racial segregation and **discrimination** called apartheid. Apartheid consisted of a series of laws that **codified** the separation of the races and steadily diminished the rights of nonwhites. The Population Registration Act of 1950 and its later amendments classified all South Africans by race, labeling them "Bantu" (black Africans), "Coloured" (mixed race), "Asian" (which included people from India and Pakistan), or "White." White people made up less than twenty percent of the population. Additional legislation prevented nonwhites from using public facilities, stripped them of their voting rights, and barred all South Africans from marrying across racial lines. It was also illegal to organize or protest against any of these laws.

In 1959, the Promotion of Bantu Self-Government Act created ten Bantu homelands, known as "townships" or "Bantustans." The government then forcibly removed black South Africans from rural areas designated as white and sent them to live in the Bantustans, while their land was sold at low prices to white farmers. From 1961 to 1994, millions of black people were ejected from their homes into Bantustans and poverty.

In 1976, an estimated twenty thousand students protested in the black township of Soweto. The students were protesting what they viewed as inferior and racist education as well as laws that forced them to learn Afrikaans, a Dutch-based African language, along with English in classrooms. Police fired on the young people with tear gas and bullets, and close to 200 protestors died. The **massacre** received intense media attention around the world. The United Nations openly condemned South Africa's apartheid policies. Many countries around the world **boycotted** South African goods. In the United States, protests against apartheid took root on college campuses. Once athletes like Arthur Ashe and singers such as Bruce Springsteen spoke out against apartheid and called for

The crowd at a 1976 South African soccer match raises its fists in the black-power salute.

sports and entertainment boycotts, even more citizens of the world rallied to force an end to apartheid.

In 1944, a young Bantu lawyer named Nelson Mandela joined a group called the African National Congress, which worked to end apartheid. In 1962, he was arrested and charged with attempting to overthrow the government, then sentenced to life in prison. As the world learned more about Mandela, politicians, authors, entertainers—and perhaps most inspiring, schoolchildren—from all over the world pleaded for him to be set free.

Nelson Mandela on a 1994 South African stamp.

Under tremendous international pressure, South Africa's president, P. W. Botha, was forced aside in 1989 in favor of F. W. de Klerk. De Klerk repealed the Population Registration Act and other apartheid legislation, and released Mandela from prison in 1990. A new constitution took effect in 1994, and Mandela was elected as president of a **coalition** government with a nonwhite majority, marking the official end of apartheid. Mandela and de Klerk jointly won the 1993 Nobel Peace Prize for their efforts ending apartheid. Mandela died in 2013 at age ninety-five in Johannesburg, South Africa.

CHAPTER SIX

ASHE VS. CONNORS

By 1975, Arthur's ranking had slipped to number five, and people began to wonder if championing causes off the court had made Arthur less of a champion on it. Ever quiet and dignified, Arthur didn't talk to the newspapers or go on television shows to defend himself. He decided to tell the critics he was still a strong competitor in his own way—on the courts, at Wimbledon.

Arthur was not favored to win the tournament. He was thirty-one, past peak age in the sport, and the previous year he had lost early in the third round. He would have to triumph over younger, stronger players such as Sweden's Björn Borg. But just as he had when he was younger, Arthur practiced hard and kept his focus on the game. One by one, round by round, he defeated

the younger players, including Borg. Focused and determined, Arthur made it to the finals. There he would face his toughest rival—American Jimmy Connors.

Twenty-two-year-old Jimmy Connors was the number-one player in the world and the defending Wimbledon champ. The lefty had bested Arthur three times before, and Arthur knew skill alone wouldn't be enough to overcome the younger man's speed and power.

Arthur studied Jimmy's game just as he had studied his opponents in the past. Jimmy had beaten Arthur in the men's finals of the 1973 South African Open, the tournament Arthur had fought so hard to enter. Before that match Arthur had written about Jimmy in his journal.

"My best strokes go to his weaknesses. My backhand is stronger than his forehand, so I'll play him down the line a lot, or right down

> "My best strokes go to his weaknesses."

the middle and refuse to give him the angles he likes. Also, because he likes to work with speed, I'll try to vary the pace on my shots. I expect to attack him on my second serve and **lob** him because his overhead is lacking."

Even though Arthur lost the match to Jimmy in 1973, Jimmy's weak spots were still the same. Arthur simply needed to hone his game plan. Leading up to the Wimbledon men's final, Arthur paid close attention to Jimmy's matches against Mexican Raúl Ramirez and American Roscoe Tanner in the quarterfinal and semifinal rounds.

Ramirez tried to outwit Connors but seemed to switch strategies partway through the match. *He had the right idea but he changed his game*, Arthur thought. Tanner was a **dynamic** player who tried to use his power against Jimmy. "Watching Roscoe told me how not to play against [Connors]," Arthur said. "I knew that I had to be restrained in my game."

Arthur decided to use his intellect as much as

his body on the court. Instead of trying to outrun, outhit, and outpower Jimmy, Arthur resolved to make Jimmy beat *himself.*

The match between Arthur and Jimmy was also personal. Opposites in almost everything, the two were adversaries off the court too. Arthur was calm and dignified. Jimmy was loud and brash. Arthur avoided the **limelight** and playing to the crowd. Jimmy loved attention and making a scene. Arthur was a team player. Jimmy was a one-man show. Worst of all in Arthur's mind was that Jimmy, as an amateur, had refused to play for the United States in the Davis Cup. Arthur said that decision "seemed unpatriotic." Furious, Jimmy had sued Arthur for millions of dollars.

As the Wimbledon final approached, each man prepared for the upcoming clash true to form. Arthur kept calm. He practiced and reviewed the strategy he would use against Jimmy. Jimmy made light of the match, practicing half-heartedly and joking with other players about Arthur's game.

CHAPTER SEVEN
WIMBLEDON, 1975

On Saturday, July 5, 1975, Arthur and Jimmy took the Centre Court. From the start, Arthur **exasperated** Jimmy with serves that hooked just out of reach. Arthur raced to the net to return Jimmy's rocket-fast ground strokes, using a **deft** touch with volleys to soften their speed and rob them of their power.

Arthur kept the ball low when Jimmy preferred it high. He hit the ball gently over the net, forcing Jimmy to burn his own strength and energy racing to meet it. Arthur won the first set, 6–1, in nineteen minutes. He won the second set, 6–1, almost as quickly.

As the match went on, hotheaded Jimmy became more and more flustered. Sweat flew from the hair fringing his face. His cheeks turned bright red. He yelled curses and angrily threw his towel under the umpire's chair.

Jimmy's **antics** didn't bother Arthur. During changeovers, when the players switched sides of the court, Arthur would sit for a minute with his eyes closed and relax. Just as Dr. Johnson had taught him, Arthur remained calm and focused, never losing his cool.

Arthur's wits and grace countered Jimmy's raw, **instinctive** power. Jimmy attacked each shot wildly, looking so **ferocious** that it seemed as if he might hurl his racket. He even shouted at the crowd. But after losing two sets in a row,

Jimmy battled back in the third, rallying to win the set.

When Jimmy took the lead in the fourth set, Arthur got a little nervous. He wondered if his plan was backfiring. Still, Arthur decided to stick with it and keep giving Jimmy short returns and angled volleys to tire him out. The two champions battled, but only one could win. Would it be the loud kid or the old bow and arrow?

Steadily Arthur regained control of the fourth set. Only one point stood between him and the championship, and it was his serve. Arthur was older, and not as strong as Jimmy, but his serve still had the power to **intimidate**. Arthur tossed the ball high. He drew back his racket arm and released it fast in a hard, sharp snap.

Jimmy lunged. His two-handed return flew back over the net. But there, waiting for it, was Arthur. He delivered a sweeping overhead smash, blasting the ball far out of Jimmy's reach.

Arthur won!

He was the first African American man to win Wimbledon. He'd also claimed the number-one world ranking, and he'd done it by playing one of the cleverest and most **exhilarating** tennis matches ever.

After the match, Arthur calmly shook Jimmy's hand. Then he toweled off his face and slipped into the Davis Cup jacket he'd worn to the court. As the crowd roared wildly, Arthur raised his arms to greet them, allowing a small smile to grace his face. With his own quiet strength, Arthur had proven he was still a powerful force.

CHAPTER EIGHT
ALWAYS A CHAMPION

In the years following his Wimbledon win, Arthur Ashe's competitive tennis career began to wind down. He became more devoted to his life off the court, and on February 20, 1977, he married a beautiful photographer named Jeanne Marie Moutoussamy. On December 12, 1986, they welcomed a daughter, naming her Camera Elizabeth.

In 1979, at the age of thirty-six, Arthur had a heart attack following a tennis clinic in New York City. Surgery fixed the problem, but his competition days were over. Being named captain of the US Davis Cup tennis team eased Arthur's move off the courts. He led his team to victories in 1981 and 1982. After he stopped coaching in 1984, he became a tennis commentator for

ABC and HBO and co-chairperson of the Player Development Committee of the United States Tennis Association (USTA), the organization he helped create in 1968 to promote inner-city junior players. Arthur also wrote *A Hard Road to Glory*, a three-book history of African American athletes.

Arthur's health continued to trouble him. He went to the hospital one day in 1988 after experiencing numbness in his right hand. After many tests, he found that he had HIV, the **virus** that causes AIDS. Doctors believed the infection came from a blood **transfusion** Arthur had received during a second heart surgery. Arthur had overcome chicken pox, measles, mumps, whooping cough, and **diphtheria** as a child. He knew that he wouldn't overcome HIV/AIDS, but he refused to let his illness break his spirit or stop him from pursuing the causes he promoted. He said, "If I were to say, 'God, why me?' about the bad things, then I should have said, 'God, why me?' about the good things that happened in my life."

HIV and AIDS

Human immunodeficiency virus infection (HIV) and acquired immune deficiency syndrome (AIDS)—more commonly known as HIV/AIDS—is a **spectrum** of conditions caused by a virus that spreads primarily through the exchange of bodily fluids between an infected person and a noninfected one. Many bodily fluids, such as saliva and tears, do not transmit HIV. AIDS was first recognized by the Centers for Disease Control in 1981. Its cause, HIV infection, first began spreading along the trade routes of the Congo Basin in Africa in the 1920s. The disease in humans likely came from chimpanzees carrying the simian immunodeficiency virus (SIV), a virus very closely related to HIV. It is believed that human beings contracted the virus by eating the flesh of chimps infected by SIV, or by infected blood coming into contact with wounds on humans who were hunting and slaughtering the animals.

Because HIV/AIDS impacted predominantly gay men in its earliest days, there was little public and political outcry to fund research to discover treatment or a cure for the disease. It was thought that only gay men could contract or sicken from HIV, and many sick people kept their status secret for fear of losing their jobs, homes, friends, and even their families. When Arthur Ashe, a straight, well-respected, and popular athlete, revealed he contracted the disease through a blood transfusion, the public came to realize that HIV wasn't a **scourge** meant to punish or wipe out a specific group of people. Ashe's admission encouraged other celebrities, politicians, and ordinary citizens to share their status and prompted more research into treating and curing the virus.

HIV/AIDS is considered a pandemic—a disease outbreak present over a large area that continues to spread. By 2014, AIDS had caused an estimated 35 million deaths worldwide. There is no cure or vaccine for HIV and AIDS. However, treatment can slow the course of the disease and possibly lead to a near-normal life expectancy.

Arthur joined other famous African Americans on a trip to South Africa in 1991 to witness the ending of apartheid. And in 1992, he became a champion for AIDS patients. That same year, *USA Today* told him they planned to run a story announcing he had HIV/AIDS. Arthur thought his health issues should be his own private business. Not wanting his daughter to find out he was sick from a newspaper article, he decided to reveal his illness to the world in his own way. On April 8, Arthur stood before reporters and television cameras and said, "Some of you heard that I had tested positive for HIV, the virus that causes AIDS. That is indeed the case."

People from all walks of life praised Arthur's courage. He was grateful for their compassion, and he kept fighting to raise research funds and awareness for HIV/AIDS. Arthur spoke to world leaders at the United Nations. He asked them to spend more money on AIDS education and finding a cure. He wanted to make sure people knew enough about the disease to keep from getting it and to stop being afraid of people who had it.

Ashe is arrested in Washington, D.C., protesting the deportation of Haitian refugees.

Arthur continued to champion other causes as well. On September 9, 1992, twenty-four years to the day after his US Open victory, Arthur was arrested outside the White House for protesting America's poor treatment of Haitian refugees. *Sports Illustrated* named Arthur its "Sportsman of the Year" in its December 1992 issue.

Two months later, on February 6, 1993, Arthur Robert Ashe Jr. died of AIDS-related pneumonia.

He was forty-nine years old. Thousands of people lined up to say good-bye to him at the governor's mansion in Richmond, Virginia. More than five thousand people attended his funeral.

Even after his death, Arthur continued to be a pioneer for **integration**. On July 10, 1996, a statue of Arthur was dedicated on Monument Avenue in Richmond. Amid white Confederate war heroes bearing sabers and sidearms stands the figure of Arthur Ashe, surrounded by children, raising books in his right hand and a tennis racket in his left. The rear inscription on the monument reads:

ARTHUR R. ASHE, JR.

1943-1993

WORLD CHAMPION, AUTHOR, HUMANITARIAN,

FOUNDER OF VIRGINIA HEROES INCORPORATED,

NATIVE OF RICHMOND, VIRGINIA

THIS MONUMENT WAS PLACED AT

MONUMENT AVENUE AND ROSENEATH

ROAD ON JULY 10, 1996, TO INSPIRE

CHILDREN AND PEOPLE OF ALL NATIONALITIES.

ARTHUR ASHE

Since we are surrounded by
so great a cloud of witnesses,
let us lay aside every weight, and
the sin which so easily ensnares us,
and let us run with endurance
the race that is set before us.

Hebrews 12:1

My potential is more than can be expressed within the bounds of my race or ethnic identity.

You've got to get to the stage in life where going for it is more important than winning or losing.

Every time you win, it diminishes the fear a little bit. You never really cancel the fear of losing; you keep challenging it.

Success is a journey, not a destination. The doing is usually more important than the outcome. Not everyone can be Number 1.

We must reach out our hand in friendship both to those who would befriend us and those who would be our enemy.

True heroism is remarkably sober, very undramatic. It is not the urge to surpass all others at whatever cost, but the urge to serve others at whatever cost.

Regardless of how you feel inside, always try to look like a winner. Even if you're behind, a sustained look of control and confidence can give you a mental edge that results in victory.

When bright young minds can't afford college, America pays the price.

When the right-wing demagogue Patrick Buchanan stood up at the 1992 Republican National Convention and implored those assembled to "take back our country" . . . I became more determined than ever that he should not succeed. And he will not. America is not *his* country. His vote is not more worthy than mine, nor yours when you come to vote. You must resist any group that believes it has a proprietary right to guide the ship of state.

I am with Thoreau, Gandhi, and Martin Luther King Jr. in their belief that violence achieves nothing but the destruction of the individual soul and the corruption of the state.

Often, when I think of a place, a music comes to mind: trumpets for Great Britain, violins for Austria and Germany, flutes for the Middle East, pianos for France, and finger pianos for West Africa; I think of drums for the American Indians, mandolins for Italy, castanets for Spain, cymbals for Japan, fiddles for our slave forebears. Each sound is like the signature of a place and its people. Each is a part of the harmony of the world.

Fluency of a language makes possible a depth of communication for which there is no substitute.

I have tried to keep on with my striving because this is the only hope I have of ever achieving anything worthwhile and lasting.

You are never really playing an opponent. You are playing yourself, your own highest standards, and when you reach your limits, that is real joy.

At some point, each individual is responsible for his or her fate. At some point, one cannot blame history.

Start where you are. Use what you have. Do what you can.

When my oldest sister, Kim, was twelve, she had a crush on Arthur Ashe, which is why I found myself in Mr. Ashe's presence not once but twice when I was eight years old. The first time, Kim wanted to attend an exhibition and clinic Mr. Ashe was conducting at the 138th Infantry Armory in St. Louis. Our mother dropped us off, and Kim was to supervise my sisters and me. But Kim didn't pay us any attention. She only had eyes for Mr. Ashe. Maybe she thought they were destined for each other, since he and our mother shared a July 10 birthday. Whatever his appeal, I didn't see it. He was taller and skinnier than any man I knew. Still, when Mr. Ashe spoke, his quiet, even voice managed to calm everyone in the arena, even me, a practiced jabbermouth.

When Mr. Ashe sat to sign autographs after the clinic, Kim was so shy and lovestruck that she froze. Her tense, sweaty hands shoving my shoulders were the last thing I felt before I found myself standing before Mr. Ashe. He took a black-and-white 8" x 10" photo of himself from a pile at his elbow.

"What's your name?" he asked in that alarmingly calm voice.

"Crystal," I told him. Mr. Ashe began writing on the photo.

"Could you make it out to Kim too?" I asked.

"Of course," Mr. Ashe said.

"And Kelly?" I asked. "And Joelle. And Lauren too."

Mr. Ashe smiled as he uncapped his pen again. "Who are all these people?"

"My sisters," I told him. "They're over there." I pointed to a column behind which Kim was partially hidden. Even from halfway across the room I could see the flame-red tips of her ears.

Mr. Ashe raised a hand and waved. Kim disappeared behind the column.

I thanked him for the photo and started away, but he called after me. Perhaps he'd noticed that my sisters and I were, along with him, among the very few people of color in attendance. "Do you and your sisters play tennis?" he asked.

"I don't," I told him. "But my sister Kim does."

"Good," Mr. Ashe said. "That's very good."

As I handed the photo over to Kim, I couldn't stop thinking about Mr. Ashe. He was dressed like a tennis player, and I'd just seen him play, but he seemed more like a teacher to me. His bright smile, distinctive glasses, and instructive yet warm delivery added up to a science teacher in my eight-year-old brain, not a superstar athlete.

Once we got home and Mr. Ashe's photo disappeared under Kim's pillow, I didn't think of him again until the next autograph signing Kim dragged us to, at a department store. Again I was the designated autograph retriever, and again my sisters and I were among the few people of color at the event. Things went a bit differently when I approached Mr. Ashe this time.

"Crystal, isn't it?" he said.

I felt famous. I couldn't open my mouth to speak. So I nodded. Mr. Ashe took a photo from his neat stack and began writing my name on it. Without looking up, he said, "Where's she hiding this time?"

"Who?" I said stupidly.

"Kim."

"Over by the water fountain," I said.

Mr. Ashe waved at Kim, finished writing, and shook my hand. "Good to see you again."

"My mother made us take tennis lessons at Tower Grove Park," I reported.

"Did you like it?" he asked.

"No," I admitted honestly. "But I like hitting the balls against the garage."

"That's a start," Mr. Ashe said, and laughed.

Our paths never crossed again after that afternoon. I eventually developed a love of tennis that, like Dr. Robert Walter Johnson, led me to pursue instruction in the game in my mid-twenties. On public courts I would envision myself in pristine whites, kneeling before the Royal Box on Centre Court before becoming the oldest player ever to win the women's singles title at Wimbledon.

In 1993, when Mr. Ashe died of AIDS-related pneumonia, I had a moment of appreciation for him that I'd never experienced before. I thought about the last time I'd sought his autograph and what he'd written on his photo. He'd remembered my name. And he'd remembered Kim's too. But he'd also remembered Kelly, Joelle, and Lauren, and he'd put their names on the photo without any prompting from me. Mr. Ashe, a man who had conquered a sport typically closed to people of color, who had walked with dignitaries and seen the world, remembered a little girl with pigtails who didn't like to play tennis.

Arthur Robert Ashe Jr. is remembered as a champion, a man who became a citizen of the world and who had a vast impact not only on sports but on the way people treat one another. I'll always remember him as a man who made a lasting impression on a quirky little tomboy with a passion for writing. *Days of Grace*, Mr. Ashe's final memoir, ends with words to his daughter. Given his generosity and kindness, I remain convinced that these words are a gift to us all:

"[W]herever I am when you feel sick at heart and weary of life, or when you stumble and fall and don't know if you can get up again, think of me. I will be watching and smiling and cheering you on."

TIMELINE

1943 July 10: Arthur Robert Ashe Jr. born, Richmond, Virginia.

1947 Moved with family to Brookfield Park, Richmond, Virginia.

1949 Began to play tennis.

1950 Mother, Mattie Cunningham Ashe, died.

1951 Won his first match, Brookfield Park, Richmond, Virginia.

1953 First attended Dr. Robert Walter Johnson's summer tennis camp, Lynchburg, Virginia.

1957 Became first African American to play in Maryland boys' championships.

1959 Competed in first US National Championships.

1960 Featured in *Sports Illustrated*'s "Faces in the Crowd."

Earned spot on US Junior Davis Cup team.

1961 Graduated from Sumner High School, St. Louis, Missouri.

Accepted college scholarship to University of California, Los Angeles.

1963 Competed in his first Wimbledon.

Became first African American man to play on US Davis Cup team.

Featured again in *Sports Illustrated*'s "Faces in the Crowd."

1964 Won Eastern Grass Court Championships, his first significant win on grass courts.

Received Johnston Award for excellent play and sportsmanship.

1965 Won NCAA singles and doubles titles; team win for UCLA.

1966 February 4: Honored with Arthur Ashe Day, Richmond, Virginia.

Graduated from UCLA.

Began two-year service in US Army; made assistant tennis coach at West Point.

1967 Published autobiography *Advantage Ashe*.

1968 Won US Nationals and US Open men's singles titles; became top-ranked amateur tennis player in America.

Ended two-year army service as second lieutenant.

Helped the United States to Davis Cup championship.

Cofounded United States Tennis Association (USTA) National Junior Tennis League.

1969   Helped found International Tennis Players Association (later known as Association of Tennis Professionals).

Gave up amateur status to turn professional.

1970   Launched movement to expel South Africa from Davis Cup competition because of apartheid policy.

Named a US goodwill ambassador to Africa.

Won Australian Open.

1973   Granted visa to South Africa.

Became first black man to play in South African Open.

1975   Won World Championship Tennis tournament and Wimbledon; became top-ranked tennis player in the world.

Published memoir *Arthur Ashe: Portrait in Motion.*

1977   February 20: Married professional photographer Jeanne Marie Moutoussamy.

1978   Won Pacific Southwest Championships, final tournament of career.

1979   Had heart attack and open-heart surgery.

1980 Announced retirement from competition.

1981 Accepted captaincy of US Davis Cup team, which went on to win championship.

Named national chairman of the American Heart Association.

Published *Off the Court*, an autobiography focusing on his life outside of tennis.

1982 Won second consecutive Davis Cup championship as captain.

1983 Received blood transfusion during second heart surgery.

1985 Inducted into International Tennis Hall of Fame in Newport, Rhode Island.

1986 December 21: Daughter, Camera Elizabeth, born.

1988 Published *A Hard Road to Glory: A History of the African American Athlete*; won Emmy Award for cowriting television adaptation.

Hospitalized for numbness in right hand.

Tested positive for HIV.

1992 Announced HIV-positive status during press conference.

Arrested outside White House protesting United States policy toward Haitian refugees.

Appealed to United Nations General Assembly for funding for AIDS research and public awareness.

Named *Sports Illustrated*'s "Sportsman of the Year."

1993   February 6: Died of AIDS-related pneumonia in New York at age forty-nine.

Funeral attended by more than five thousand people, Richmond, Virginia.

$500,000 raised by the Arthur Ashe Foundation for the Defeat of AIDS.

Memoir *Days of Grace* published.

Awarded Presidential Medal of Freedom by President Bill Clinton.

1996   July 10: Statue of Arthur Ashe dedicated, Monument Avenue, Richmond, Virginia.

1997   The US Tennis Association announced new US Open stadium, Arthur Ashe Stadium, National Tennis Center, Flushing, New York.

2005   US Postal Service released commemorative Arthur Ashe stamp.

GLOSSARY

aggressive (uh-GRES-iv) *adjective* eager to attack or to start a fight

amateur (AM-uh-chur) *noun* someone who participates in an activity for the fun of it rather than for pay

anticipation (an-TIS-uh-pay-shun) *noun* the act of thinking about or looking forward to an event in the future

antics (AN-tiks) *plural noun* actions or behavior meant to be silly, playful, or funny

backhand (BAK-hand) *noun* in tennis, a stroke made with the back of the hand swinging away from the body

befall (bee-FOL) *verb* to happen to

boycott (BOI-kot) *verb* to avoid doing business with a company or organization to protest its actions; *noun* the act of boycotting a place

carnation (kar-NAY-shun) *noun* a white, pink, red, or yellow flower with many small petals, often worn as a decoration for formal occasions

coalition (ko-uh-LISH-un) *noun* a group of people or smaller groups united to achieve some goal

codify (KOD-ee-fie) *verb* to organize laws or rules into an orderly system

courteous (KOR-tee-us) *adjective* polite; respectful; considerate

deft (DEFT) *adjective* fast and nimble

diphtheria (DIF-theer-ee-uh) *noun* an illness that affects the air passages of the throat, making it difficult to breathe

discrimination (dis-KRIM-uh-nay-shun) *noun* the act of treating some people better than others, usually for a prejudiced or unfair reason

dynamic (die-NAM-ik) *adjective* containing a lot of energy; active

endorsement (en-DOOR-smint) *noun* approval or support

exasperate (ek-ZAS-per-ate) *verb* to make someone annoyed or irritated

exhilarating (ek-ZIL-er-ate) *adjective* exciting, refreshing, or energizing

exploit (EK-sploit) *verb* to use something to its greatest extent

extensive (ek-STEN-siv) *adjective* wide; long; in-depth

fanfare (FAN-fare) *noun* a burst of music played by trumpets; more commonly, a splashy display or ceremony meant to attract public attention

ferocious (fuhr-OH-shus) *adjective* fierce; intense

forehand (FOR-hand) *noun* in tennis, a stroke made with the palm of the hand facing forward

gloat (GLOTE) *verb* to feel or show a selfish pleasure in your own success or someone else's failure

instinctive (in-STINK-tiv) *adjective* guided by an inner feeling or natural ability

integration (IN-tee-GRAY-shun) *noun* the act or result of combining parts into a whole; particularly the acceptance of different groups into society and institutions as equals

intimidate (in-TIM-ee-date) *verb* to make someone else afraid, especially with threats; to bully

limelight (LIME-lite) *noun* intense public attention

lob (LAWB) *verb* to strike or toss an object so it flies high in the air and falls in a smooth arc

massacre (MAS-uh-ker) *noun* the violent killing of a large number of people

precision (pree-SIZSH-un) *noun* the quality of being very careful or accurate

ranking points (RANK-ing POINTS) *noun* in tennis, the points that determine a player's rank among all current members of a competitive league. Players earn points through winning matches in tournaments.

scourge (SKERJ) *noun* something that creates a great deal of suffering

segregate (seg-ree-GATE) *verb* to separate people of different groups, particularly based on race

snub (SNUB) *noun* the act of treating someone in a rude or insulting way

spectrum (SPEK-truhm) *noun* a wide range

stamina (STAM-ee-nuh) *noun* strength or endurance

straight sets (STRATE SETS) *plural noun* winning a match in the fewest possible sets and without losing a single set

transfusion (trans-FYOO-zhun) *noun* the transfer of some fluid (usually blood) from one person to another

virus (VIE-ruhs) *noun* a tiny particle that can grow in living cells and often carries disease; also, an illness caused by a virus

AUTHOR'S SOURCES

ARTHUR ASHE

Ashe, Arthur, and Frank Deford. *Arthur Ashe: Portrait in Motion*. New York: Carroll & Graf Publishers, 1975.

Ashe, Arthur, and Arnold Rampersad. *Days of Grace*. New York: Ballantine Books, 1993.

Deford, Frank. "Service, But First a Smile." *Sports Illustrated*, August 29, 1966.

————. "The Once and Future Diplomat." *Sports Illustrated*, March 1, 1971.

Gray, David. "Arthur Ashe's blow for peace." *Manchester Guardian*, July 5, 1975.

Mantell, Paul. *Arthur Ashe: Young Tennis Champion* (Childhood of Famous Americans). New York: Aladdin, 2006.

Moore, Kenny. "Sportsman of the Year." *Sports Illustrated*, December 21, 1992.

————. "He Did All He Could." *Sports Illustrated*, February 15, 1993.

Price, S. L. "Slow Train to Eminence." *Sports Illustrated 40th Anniversary Issue*, September 19, 1994.

Steins, Richard. *Arthur Ashe: A Biography*. Santa Barbara, CA: Greenwood Press, 2005.

Towle, Mike. *I Remember Arthur Ashe: Memories of a True Tennis Pioneer and Champion of Social Causes by the People Who Knew Him*. Nashville, TN: Cumberland House Publishing, 2001.

SCORING IN TENNIS AND GRAND SLAMS

Collins, Bud. *The Bud Collins History of Tennis: An Authoritative Encyclopedia and Record Book*. Washington, DC: New Chapter Press, 2016.

ESPN. "Men's Grand Slam Title Winners." http://www.espn.com/tennis/history

ESPN. "Women's Grand Slam Title Winners." http://www.espn.com/tennis/history/_/type/women

McEnroe, Patrick and Peter Bodo. *Tennis for Dummies*. New York: Dummies Press, 1998.

Pruitt, Sarah. "Tennis' Elusive Grand Slam." History.com. Published July 2, 2015. http://www.history.com/news/tennis-elusive-grand-slam-quest

Tenniscamper.com. "Tennis Grand Slam Tournaments History." Adidas Tennis Camps. Published June 24, 2015. http://tenniscamper.com/short-history-of-the-grand-slam-tournaments/

Williams, Venus and Serena Williams. *How to Play Tennis.* New York: DK Publishing, 2004.

ALTHEA GIBSON

"Althea's Odyssey: From Harlem to High Places of Tennis." *Life Magazine.* July 2, 1956, 88–89.

Gibson, Althea. *I Always Wanted to Be Somebody.* Edited by Edward E. Fitzgerald and Stephen M. Joseph. New York: Noble and Noble, 1970.

Gray, Frances Clayton, and Yanick Rice Lamb. *Born to Win: The Authorized Biography of Althea Gibson.* John Wiley & Sons, 2004.

Miller, Rex, dir. *American Masters: Althea.* Premiered September 4, 2015 on PBS. http://www.pbs.org/wnet/americanmasters/althea-gibson-preview-althea/3927/

Preston, Mark. "Black History Month Legends: Althea Gibson." United States Tennis Association. Published February 6, 2017. https://www.usta.com/en/home/stay-current/national/black-history-month-legends--althea-gibson.html

APARTHEID

Clark, Nancy L. , and William H. Worger. *South Africa: The Rise and Fall of Apartheid.* Seminar Studies. London: Routledge/Taylor & Francis Group, 2016.

Encyclopedia Britannica Online, s.v. "Apartheid." Accessed August 2, 2017. https://www.britannica.com/topic/apartheid

Gordon, David M. *Apartheid in South Africa: A Brief History with Documents.* Bedford Cultural Editions. Boston: Bedford/St. Martin's, 2017.

Keller, Bill. "Mandela is Named President, Closing the Era of Apartheid." *New York Times*, May 9, 1994.

HIV AND AIDS

Gallant, Joel E. *100 Questions and Answers About HIV and AIDS*, 3rd ed. Burlington, MA: Jones & Bartlett Learning, 2015.

Sepkowitz, Kent A., MD. "AIDS — The First 20 Years." *New England Journal of Medicine*, 344 (June 7, 2001): 1764-1772.

Vergel, Nelson. "There When AIDS Began: An Interview with Michael Gottlieb, MD." The Body: The Complete AIDS/HIV Resource. Published June 2, 2011. http://www.thebody.com/content/62330/there-when-aids-began-an-interview-with-michael-go.html

RECOMMENDED FURTHER READING

TENNIS

Nonfiction

Braun, Kevin. *Tennis for the 10 & Under: The New Look of Tennis from A to Z.* Kansas City, MO: Big Bird Creative, 2016.

Christopher, Matt. *Serena Williams.* Matt Christopher Legends in Sports. New York: Little, Brown Books for Young Readers, 2017.

Drewett, Jim. *How to Improve at Tennis.* St. Catherine's, ON, Canada: Crabtree, 2008.

Gitlin, Marty. *The Best Tennis Players of All Time.* Sports' Best Ever. Edina, MN: Sportszone/Abdo, 2015.

Savage, Jeff. *Roger Federer.* Amazing Athletes. Minneapolis: First Avenue Editions/Lerner, 2009.

Schuh, Mari. *Andy Murray.* Famous Athletes. Mankato, MN: Capstone, 2016.

Stauffacher, Sue. *Nothing but Trouble: The Story of Althea Gibson.* Illustrated by Greg Couch. New York: Knopf Books for Young Readers, 2007.

Fiction

Feinstein, John. *Vanishing Act: Mystery at the U.S. Open.* The Sports Beat. New York: Knopf Books for Young Readers, 2006.

Johnson, Varian. *The Parker Inheritance.* New York: Arthur A. Levine Books/Scholastic, 2018.

APARTHEID

Nonfiction

Barfield, Cecilia, and Gill Gordon, eds. *All About South Africa: Our Country, Its People, History, Cultures, Economy and Wildlife.* Johannesburg, South Africa: Penguin Random House South Africa, 2016.

Denenberg, Barry. *Nelson Mandela: "No Easy Walk to Freedom."* New York: Scholastic, 2014.

Erskine, Kathryn. *Mama Africa!: How Miriam Makeba Spread Hope with Her Song.* Illustrated by Charly Palmer. New York: FSG Books for Young Readers, 2017.

Nelson, Kadir. *Nelson Mandela.* New York: Katherine Tegen Books/HarperCollins, 2013.

Fiction

Bildner, Phil. *The Soccer Fence: A Story of Friendship, Hope and Apartheid in South Africa.* Illustrated by Jesse Joshua Watson. New York: G.P. Putnam's Sons Books for Young Readers, 2014.

HIV & AIDS

Nonfiction

Giblin, James Cross. *When Plague Strikes: The Black Death, Smallpox, AIDS.* Illustrations by David Frampton. New York: HarperCollins, 1995.

Raum, Elizabeth. *I Know Someone with HIV/AIDS.* Understanding Health Issues. Mankato, MN: Capstone, 2011.

Rawl, Paige, with Ali Benjamin. *Positive: A Memoir.* New York: HarperCollins, 2014.

Fiction

Sheinmel, Courtney. *Positively.* New York: Simon & Schuster Books for Young Readers, 2009.

ABOUT THE AUTHOR AND ILLUSTRATOR

CRYSTAL HUBBARD is a sports buff and full-time writer. She is also the author of the Lee & Low books *The Last Black King of the Kentucky Derby*, about jockey Jimmy "Wink" Winkfield, and *Catching the Moon: The Story of A Young Girl's Baseball Dreams*, about Marcenia Lyle, the first woman to play for an all-male professional baseball team. She says, "It's important for me to tell the stories of African-American and female heroes because they are ordinary people who do extraordinary things, and their stories too often go untold." Hubbard lives in St. Louis, Missouri with her family.

KEVIN BELFORD is an illustrator and fine artist whose work has been featured in books, newspapers, magazines, and advertisements. He also wrote and illustrated the book *Devil at the Confluence*. A graduate of the Kansas City Art Institute, he lives in St. Louis, Missouri.